SP🐾T

HORSES

ARABIAN HORSES

by Alissa Thielges

AMICUS

coat

legs

Look for these words and pictures as you read.

 nostrils

 tail

An Arabian horse trots by.
Look at it go!

See the coat?
It has silky hair.
The skin under it is black.

coat

Arabians are tough horses.
They can run for a long time.

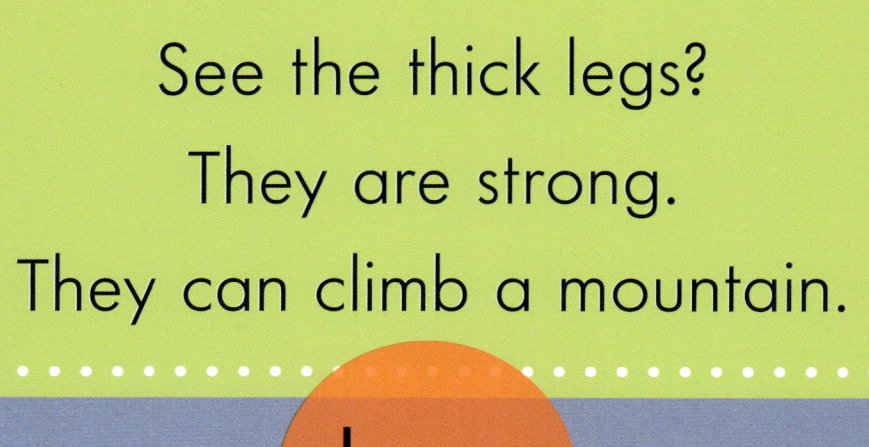

See the thick legs?
They are strong.
They can climb a mountain.

legs

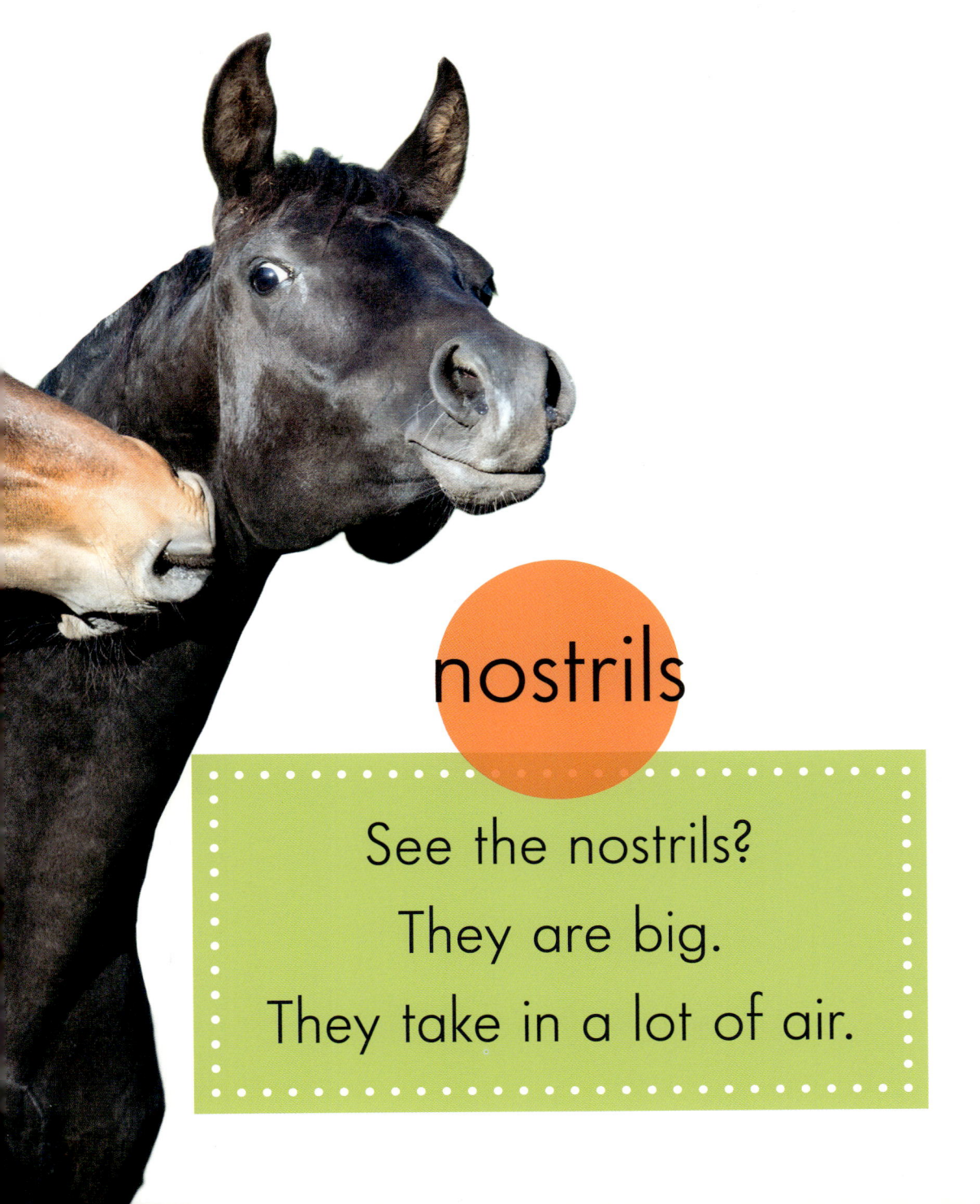

nostrils

See the nostrils?
They are big.
They take in a lot of air.

See the long tail?
It is held high.
The horse looks beautiful.

tail

Arabian horses run fast.
They win long races.

See the coat?
It has silky hair.
The skin under it is black.

coat

coat

See the thick legs?
They are strong.
They can climb a mountain.

legs

legs

Did you find?

nostrils

See the nostrils?
They are big.
They take in a lot of air.

nostrils

See the long tail?
It is held high.
The horse looks beautiful.

tail

tail

Spot is published by Amicus
P.O. Box 227, Mankato, MN 56002
www.amicuspublishing.us

Library of Congress Cataloging-in-Publication Data
Names: Thielges, Alissa, 1995- author.
Title: Arabian horses / by Alissa Thielges.
Description: Mankato, Minnesota : Amicus, [2023] | Series:
    Spot horses | Audience: Ages 4-7 | Audience: Grades
    K-1 | Summary: "Meet the Arabian horse breed in this
    leveled reader that reinforces key vocabulary with a
    search-and-find feature that builds new vocabulary and
    creates a successful foundation for emergent readers."—
    Provided by publisher.
Identifiers: LCCN 2021055469 (print) | LCCN 2021055470
    (ebook) | ISBN 9781645492450 (hardcover) | ISBN
    9781681527697 (paperback) | ISBN 9781645493334
    (ebook)
Subjects: LCSH: Arabian horse--Juvenile literature.
Classification: LCC SF293.A8 T455 2023 (print) | LCC
    SF293.A8 (ebook) | DDC 636.1/12--dc23/eng/20211213
LC record available at https://lccn.loc.gov/2021055469
LC ebook record available at https://lccn.loc.
gov/2021055470

Rebecca Glaser, editor
Deb Miner, series designer
Catherine Berthiaume and Grant Gould,
book design and photo research

Photos by Alamy/Imagebroker, cover;
Shutterstock/Abramova Kseniya 1,
Husaineb 3, Makarova Viktoria 4-5,
Alexia Khruscheva 10-11, Makarova
Viktoria 12-13; Alamy/Juniors Bildarchiv
GmbH 6-7; Getty/marlenka 14-15;
KimballStock/Ron Kimball, 8-9

ARABIAN HORSES